HowExpert Presents

How To Speed Up Your Computer

Your Step By Step Guide To Speeding Up Your Computer

HowExpert

For more tips related to this topic, visit HowExpert.com/speedcomputer.

Recommended Resources

- HowExpert.com – Quick 'How To' Guides on All Topics from A to Z by Everyday Experts.
- HowExpert.com/free – Free HowExpert Email Newsletter.
- HowExpert.com/books – HowExpert Books
- HowExpert.com/courses – HowExpert Courses
- HowExpert.com/clothing – HowExpert Clothing
- HowExpert.com/membership – HowExpert Membership Site
- HowExpert.com/affiliates – HowExpert Affiliate Program
- HowExpert.com/writers – Write About Your #1 Passion/Knowledge/Expertise & Become a HowExpert Author.
- HowExpert.com/resources – Additional HowExpert Recommended Resources
- YouTube.com/HowExpert – Subscribe to HowExpert YouTube.
- Instagram.com/HowExpert – Follow HowExpert on Instagram.
- Facebook.com/HowExpert – Follow HowExpert on Facebook.

Publisher's Foreword

Dear HowExpert reader,

HowExpert publishes quick 'how to' guides on all topics from A to Z by everyday experts.

At HowExpert, our mission is to discover, empower, and maximize talents of everyday people to ultimately make a positive impact in the world for all topics from A to Z...one everyday expert at a time!

All of our HowExpert guides are written by everyday people just like you and me who have a passion, knowledge, and expertise for a specific topic.

We take great pride in selecting everyday experts who have a passion, great writing skills, and knowledge about a topic that they love to be able to teach you about the topic you are also passionate about and eager to learn about.

We hope you get a lot of value from our HowExpert guides and it can make a positive impact in your life in some kind of way. All of our readers including you altogether help us continue living our mission of making a positive impact in the world for all spheres of influences from A to Z.

If you enjoyed one of our HowExpert guides, then please take a moment to send us your feedback from wherever you got this book.

Thank you and we wish you all the best in all aspects of life.

Sincerely,

BJ Min
Founder & Publisher of HowExpert
HowExpert.com

PS...If you are also interested in becoming a HowExpert author, then please visit our website at HowExpert.com/writers. Thank you & again, all the best!

Table of Contents

Chapter 1: Computers

Introduction

Due to their wide range of applications, computers are used in virtually all aspects of daily living in today's technology filled world. Globalization requires users to keep up to date with the latest technological advances in computing hardware and software.

Computers are considered an integral part of life as they make work easier and faster in a highly efficient manner. They are able to process a tremendous amount of data with accuracy.

Computers are classified as "analog", "digital" or "hybrid" based upon their operating principles. Computers are also categorized as microcomputers, mini Computers, medium-size computers, large computers and super computers based upon their capacity.

A personal computer (PC) is a household item, operated by an individual either at home or at an office. A PC can be either "desktop" or "laptop" and will have various types of installed software according to the user's requirements.

History

No single person can be credited with the invention of the computer. In fact, the computer has been created through the mutual contributions and efforts of innovative and revolutionary thinking scientists, mathematicians, philosophers and engineers.

The first electrical binary programmable computer Z1 was created by Germany's Konrad Zuse during 1936-1938. In 1946, the first digital computer ENIAC was invented by the US Army. It weighed approximately 50 tons, was powered by 18,000 vacuum tubes and was capable of solving almost all mathematical problems.

In 1971, the first PC named "Kenback-1" was introduced. Later on, in 1975, Ed Roberts introduced another personal computer   "Altair 8800".

Chapter 2: What The Guide Focuses On

Computers are incredible devices capable of performing multiple data processing and communication functions. However, these devices do require periodic maintenance to perform efficiently. This guide will teach you step-by-step how to significantly speed up your computer. Some of the tactics mentioned in this guide work with specific versions of the Windows OS. However, most of them work well with all the operating system with few variations.

Most of these tactics use utilities which are already built into the Windows Operating System. You may make use of these utilities as often as you like, without charge, to maintain the performance of your PC.

Chapter 3: How To Speed Up Windows 7

How To Remove Unwanted Programs

Users will often install multiple programs to fulfill their needs. These programs must be removed when they are no longer needed as they take up valuable space and noticeably decrease the speed of the computer.

To remove the unwanted programs, the following two tactics need to be taken:

<u>*Tactic 1:*</u>

Click on the **Start** button and navigate the mouse to the control Panel.

Select the **Programs and Features** icon.

Select any program and click the **Uninstall Program** button to disable it.

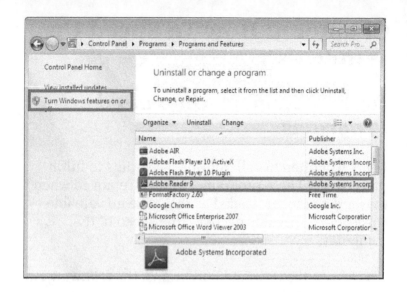

Uninstall or Change Program Window

Alternatively, the **Turn Window Features on or off** may be used to serve the same purpose.

Tactic 2:

Click on **Start** button at bottom left hand corner.

Move to the **Control Panel** icon.

Click **Add or Remove** Program. Windows will compile a list of programs against how often you use it and when it was last time used.

Remove the entire unnecessary program that you are not using or don't have plans to use in the future.

Note: Do not delete any program labeled as an update or hot fix. You may be required to restart the computer before programs are completely deleted.

How To Defragment The Hard Drive

If you are using your computer for a long period of time, the hard disk will become fragmented which may slow down the computer.

Windows can defragment the computer with the following two methods:

From My Computer

Click on **My Computer** icon, placed on computer's desktop.

Right click on **Hard Drive** (By default the letter C is used for Hard Drive), and select **Properties**.

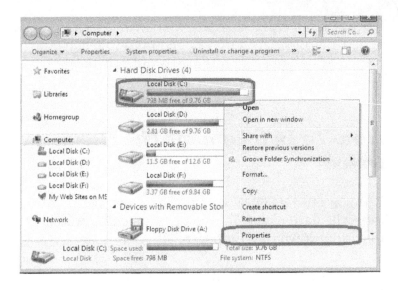

Computer Window

Select the **Tools** tab.

Click on **Defragment Now**.

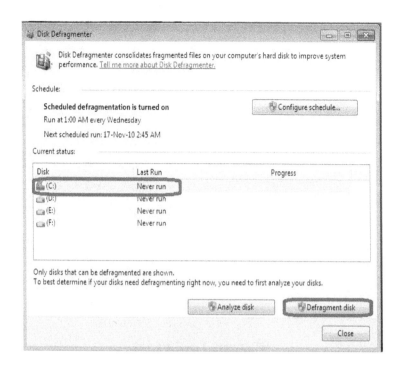

Disk Defragmenter

From The Start Menu

Click the Start button.

Select the All Programs folder.

Select the Accessories and then click on System Tools.

Click on the Disk Defragmenter application.

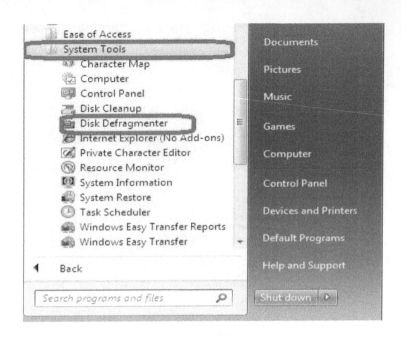

System Tools List

From the opening window, select the hard disk you want to clean up and then click **"Defragment"**.

Remove PC Junk

PC junk can be in any form such as; temporary internet files, offline web pages, files in the recycle bin or compressed old files. To remove these files, Disk Cleanup utility is used.

To find Disk Cleanup in Windows, following steps needs to follow:

Click **Start.**

From the menu, click **All Programs.**

Select **Accessories** and then expand **System Tools.**

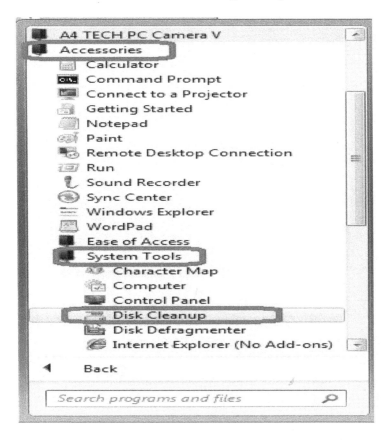

Accessories Sub list

Click on **Disk Cleanup**.

Disk Cleanup

From the dialog box, select the drive that need to be cleaned and then click **OK**.

Turn Off Visual Effects

Users can enhance the performance of their computers by disabling some of the visual effects on Windows. There are approximately twenty visual effects that may be controlled by the user.

Users are able to adjust the visual effects from the Performance Option dialog box as mentioned below:

Click on **Start** button and then move to **Control Panel.**

Click **System and Maintenance** and then select **Performance Information and Tools**.

Select the **Visual Effects**.

Select **Adjust for Best Performance** and click **OK.**

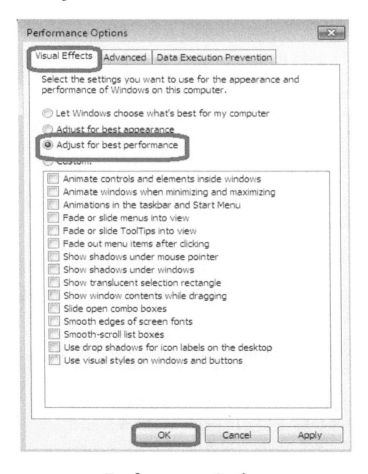

Performance Option

Note: A less drastic option would be for the user to select Let **Windows choose what's best for my computer**. If the system prompts for an administrator password then the visual effects may be adjusted after typing the password.

Disable The Search Indexing Feature

The Search Indexing feature offered specifically in Windows 7 is used to keep records of files in order to trace them easily when requested. This service is particularly helpful for frequent computer searches. For infrequent searchers, it is recommended to disable this option as it requires a large amount of space.

Follow the stated steps below to disable the search indexing service:

On the desktop, Right click the **Computer icon**.

Select **Manage, Computer Management window will open.**

Click **Services and Applications and then choose Services.**

From the long-appeared list of services, select Window Searches. In result, Window Search Properties window open.

From Startup Type, select Disabled from menu and click **OK.**

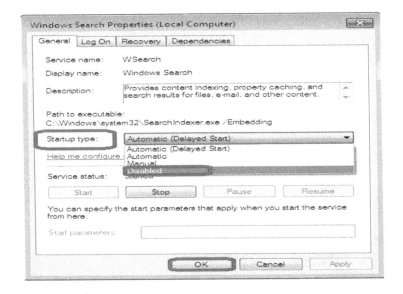

Windows Search Properties

Disable Undesired System Sounds

All versions of Windows OS are equipped with multiple sound effects which a user will be able to hear while interacting with computer. By default, these sound effects utilize the system resources.

To disable the unwanted system sounds, following steps are followed:

Type "**mmsys.cpl**" in **Run** dialog box and press enter.

Move to the **Sounds** tab.

Under the **Sound Scheme** option, choose **No Sounds** and press Ok.

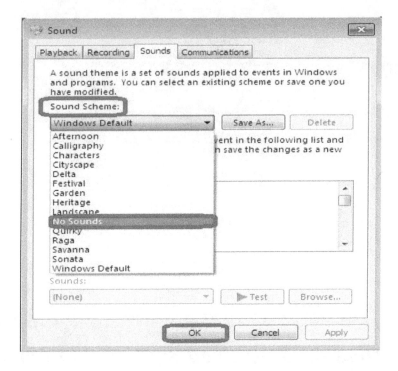

Sound Dialog box

Note: Experts suggest that sounds played during the Windows Start up, Shutdown, Logon, etc should necessarily be disabled to noticeably enhance the speed of computer.

Disable Unwanted Start Up Items

When a computer starts up, many unnecessary software programs will run which ultimately result in slowing down the system. Even as older programs are replaced or no longer needed, they continue to operate and consume system resources, slowing down the overall speed and function of the computer.

To prevent such services from starting which also saves time during Windows startups, the following steps are suggested:

From the Start menu, Click on the Run option.

Type the code "**msconfig**" in Run dialog box and press Enter to open **System Configuration Utility.**

Select the **Startup** tab. Uncheck the entries that are not needed from the available list.

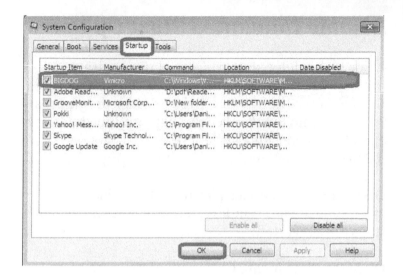

System Configuration

Turn Off Windows Screen Savers And Wallpapers

A screen saver is a moving picture or pattern and appears when the computer has not been used for a specified time. Wallpapers are the images displayed on the desktop. Systems require memory to display both the screen saver and wallpaper.

Users are able to preserve megabytes by disabling these two features of Windows as stated below:

How To Disable The Screen Saver:

Right Click on **Computer Desktop** and select **Personalize.**

Click the **Screen Saver** link and from the drop-down list, set it to **None.**

Click **Apply** and then press **Ok.**

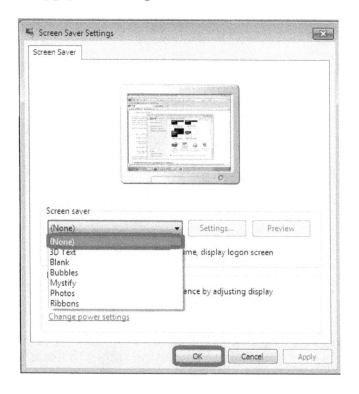

Screen Saver Settings

How To Reset Desktop Background:

Right click on the **Desktop** and select **Personalize.**

Navigate to **Desktop Background** link. Select the **Solid Colors** from the **Location** drop down menu.

Choose one color of your choice and select **OK.**

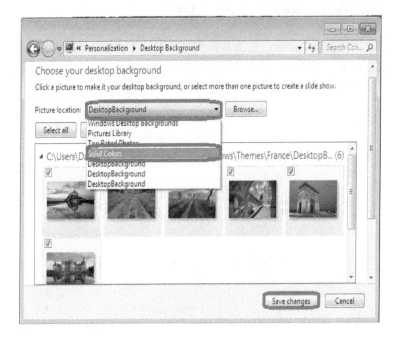

Note: It is suggested to use a desktop background that is lower in size and resolution rather to use a single color for it.

Disable The Aero Peek And Aero Snap Feature

Aero Peek equips the system with the power of X-ray vision so that all the past opened windows can be peered directly to the desktop. Additionally, Aero Snap assists you in resizing the window just by dragging and dropping it into the screen corners.

Users may disable both features by following the understated steps to maximize the speed of their system:

How To Disable the Aero Peek

- Click on the **Windows** icon placed on the desktop and navigate to the **Control Panel.**
- Double click on **Ease of Access Center** icon. Select the **Make it easier to focus on tasks** option.
- Uncheck the box **Prevent windows from being automatically arranged when moved to the edge of the screen.**

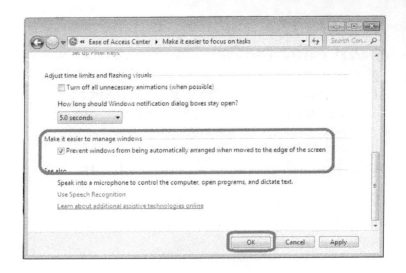

Aero Peek

How To Disable The Aero Snap

Right click the **Windows taskbar** and choose **Properties.**

From the **Taskbar** tab, uncheck the option **Use Aero Peek to preview the desktop.**

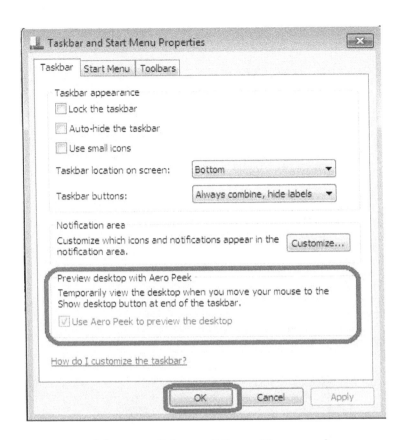

Taskbar and Start Menu Properties

Disable User Account Control Utility

The UAC or User Account Control utility protects the computer from harmful viruses. But it may be annoying for the advanced user or regular users because it causes the system to slow down considerably:

How To Disable The UAC

- Open the **Control Panel** and then select the **User Accounts and Family Safety** option.
- Select **User Account Control Setting** and pull the slider towards the option **Never Notify**.
- Click **OK** and restart your computer system.

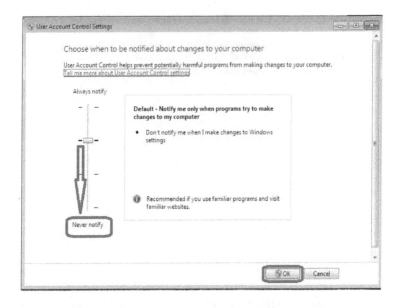

User Account Control Settings

Remove Undesired Fonts

All the versions of Window operating system offer a range of font options. It is suggested to reduce this font list and limits it to some basic and frequently used fonts to free some resources for optimal performance.

How To Remove The Unnecessary Fonts

Click on the **Start** button and open **Control Panel.**

Click on the **Fonts Folder.**

Move unnecessary fonts to a temporary folder to call them back when needed or permanently delete them.

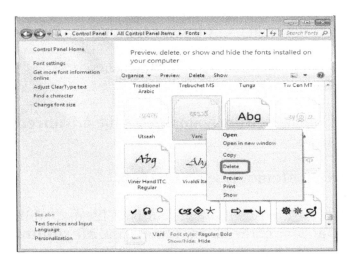

Fonts List

Note: Experts suggest being careful not to delete the folders as some of the fonts which are useless for you may be required to execute system processes.

Optimize Page Filing Of The System

By default, many updated versions of Windows OS set the page file size to 1.5X the amount of physical memory. Experts suggest changing the page file size ratio 1:1 to physical memory size if the PC has more than 512MB of memory.

How To Change The Size Of The Page Files

Right click on **My Computer** and click **Properties**.

Select the **Advanced** tab and then choose **Performance** tab.

Click on the **Setting** button. Select the **Advanced** tab again.

 Virtual Memory, select **Change.**

Select the drive containing your page file and set the **Initial Size** of the file the same as the **Maximum Size** of the file.

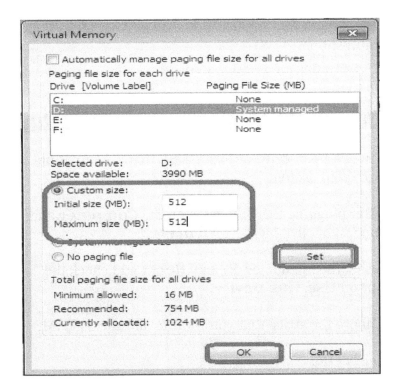

Virtual Memory Settings

Note: If the user sets a fixed size for the page file then it does not require to OS to resize the page file again and again.

Set Up The Ready Boost Services

Computer users may select the ready boost to enhance the performance of the computer by using the flesh drive or pen drive or USB drive as RAM. In general, professional users utilize the ready boost utility for launching bulky applications such as Adobe Photoshop.

How To Utilize The Ready Boost Utility

Choose a pen drive or Flash/USB that is compatible with your system.

After plugging the USB, click on the **Computer** and then right click on the **USB drive.**

Select the tab named **Ready Boost** and check the option **Use This Device.**

Choose the space that you want to allocate as RAM.

Select **OK.**

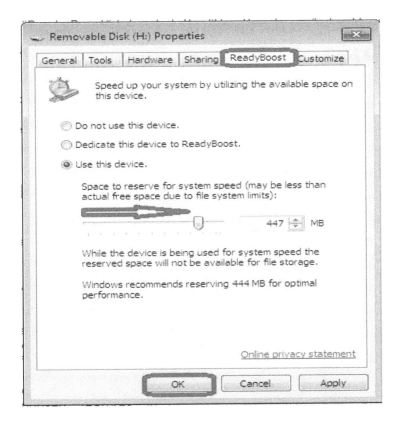

Removable Disk Properties

Turn Off Desktop Gadgets

Although Windows 7 detached the actual visual sidebar of Windows Vista there are still some of the sidebar processes running which might affect the performance of your system.

How To Turn Off Operating System's Extras

Click on the **Start** button and type **"gadgets"** in the search box of start menu.

Choose "**View list of running gadgets**".

In the next opening windows, select each gadget in turn and click on **Remove** to close the selected unused gadgets in their entirety.

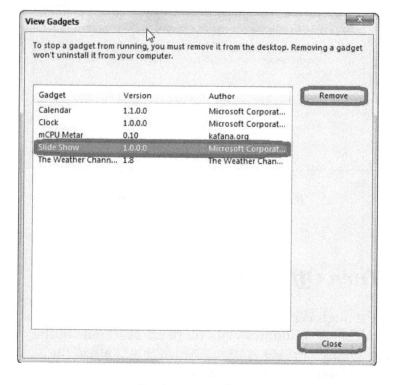

Gadget Settings

Update Drivers And Windows

A driver is the software used by the Windows to configure hardware devices. The Windows update application is used to automatically check for updated versions of the Windows operating systems and its basic drivers.

The drivers used by the computers are normally specific to its peripherals, thus the update process may be slightly different for each user. A good general guideline is for users to follow the manufacturer's instructions.

How To Update The Drivers And Windows OS

Tactic 1:

Click on **Start** button.

Select **All Programs** and open **Windows Update** from the sub-list.

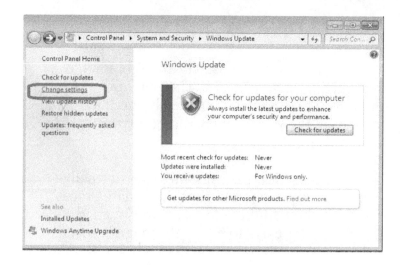

Windows Update Settings

Click on **Change Setting** which will enable you to choose the way you want to install the update.

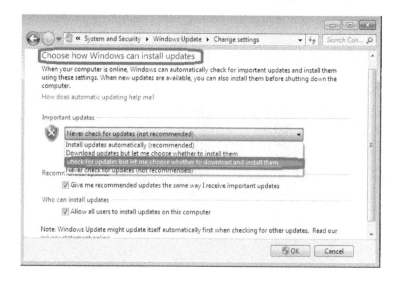

Change Settings for Windows Updates

Tactic 2:

Click the **Start** button from the **Task Bar.**

Select **Control Panel** and click on **Automatic Updates**.

From the opening window, select **Automatic.**

Detect And Repair Disk Errors

To optimize the performance of computer, it is necessary to check the hard drive for bad sectors and errors which may slow down the system. Windows OS provides the Error Checking Utility to ensure the integrity of files stored on the hard disk.

It is suggested to use the Error Checking utility once a week to prevent errors or data loss.

How To Run The Error Checking Utility

- Click on the **Start** menu after closing all the open applications or files.
- Click on the **Computer** and from the computer window, right click the hard disk that needs to be scanned for bad sectors.
- Click **Properties** and then click on **Tools** Tab.

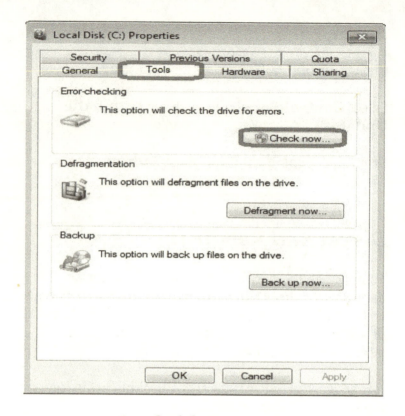

Local Disk Properties

- Select the **Check Now** option, in the check disk window, Select the **Scan for and attempt recovery of bad sectors** check box and then **Start.**

If bad sectors are identified, select to fix them.

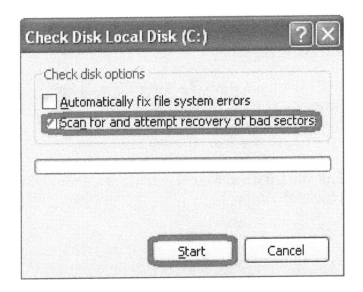

Check Disk Options

Note: If you think that the hard disk contains errors, you can select the **Automatically fix file system errors.**

Reset Recycle Bin To 1-3 Percent Of Hard Drive

In all the versions of Microsoft OS, the Recycle Bin is used as a holding space for files and folders before final deletion from the storage device. By default, the Recycle Bin requires too much space.

How To Reduce The Storage Space Of Recycle Bin

Right Click on the **Recycle Bin** placed on the desktop.

Select **Properties** from the drop-down list.

Reduce the **Custom Size** down to a lesser amount and click **OK**.

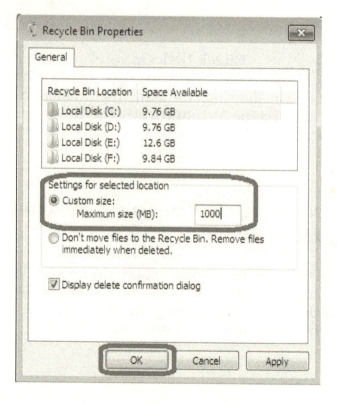

Recycle Bin Properties

Disable The Thumbnail Preview Feature

The thumbnail feature in Windows 7 shows a small thumbnail of the folders instead of their icons. Users are able save system resources for quicker browsing by disabling the thumbnail feature.

How To Disable The Thumbnail Feature

Double click the **Computer** icon placed on the desktop.

Select the **Organize** drop down menu and select the **Folder and Search option.**

Navigate to the **View** tab in the opening window and enable the option **Always show icons, never thumbnails.**

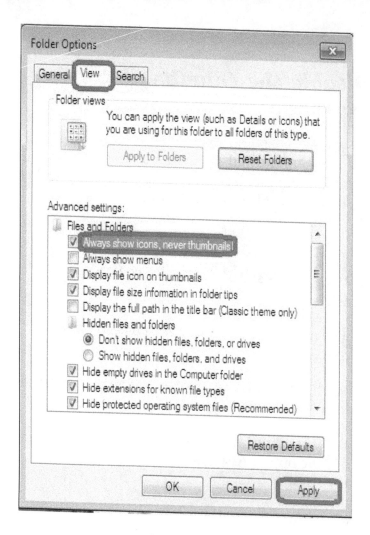

Folder Option

Click **Apply** and click **OK.**

Change The Power Plan To Maximum Performance

By default, the power plan of Windows 7 is set for balanced performance. You may optimize the performance of your computer by selecting the "High Performance" plan which may consume slightly more energy.

How To Set The High Performance Plan For Your Computer

From the **Control Panel,** Double click on **Power Option.**

Click on the down arrow presenting the option **Show Additional Plans** to select the **High Performance Power Plan**.

Check the **High Performance Plan.**

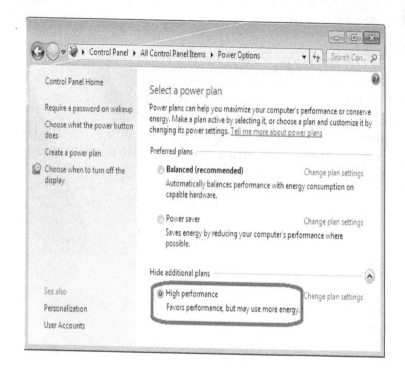

Power Options

Note: For more optimized performance, users may make **choices** from **Advanced Settings.**

Performance Troubleshooter

Windows offers a Troubleshooter utility in its updated version to enhance the performance of the system after automatically finding and fixing the problems which cause the system to slow down.

How To Run The Troubleshooter

Click on the **Start** button and move to the **Control Panel.**

Type **Troubleshooting** in the control panel's search box.

Under **System and Security,** select the option "**Check for Performance Issues**".

Run the troubleshooter to find and fix the root reason for the slower system.

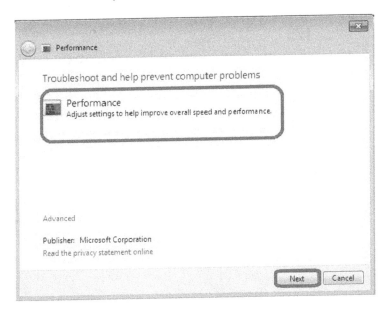

Troubleshoot and help prevent computer problems

Performance
Adjust settings to help improve overall speed and performance.

Advanced

Publisher: Microsoft Corporation
Read the privacy statement online

Next   Cancel

Performance Option

Disable Windows Defender

Windows Defender acts as a first line of defense against spyware, malware and other unwanted software. If the user is relying on third party software like Norton, AVG and MacAfee for security purposes, it is suggested to close windows defender which will free computer resources which will ultimately result in enhanced performance.

How To Disable The Windows Defender

- Right click the **Computer** icon on the desktop and choose **Manage.**
- Click on the **Services and Applications** tab.
- Select the **Services** option and from the next opening window, scroll down the list and right click on the **Windows Defender** option.
- Click **Stop** to disable the Windows Defender.
- The user may set the services startup type to disable to keep it from starting when the computer is rebooted.

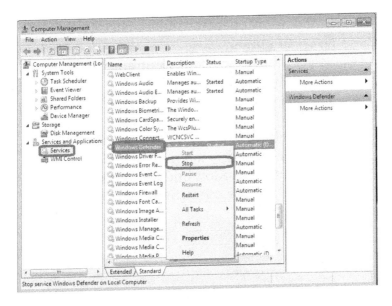

Windows Defender Option

Enable Write Caching On Device

This practice enables the OS to flush changed data to the hard disk when the system is free. In this way, the performance of the system is not affected when the system is in use.

How To Enable Write Caching On The Device:

- Click on the **Control Panel** and then select **System and Security.**

49

- In the newly opened window, click on the **System** option.
- Select the **Device Manager** and then expand the **Disk Drives.**
- The drop-down list shows the hard drive of the system. Right click on it and select **Properties.**
- Click the **Policies** tab in the **Device Properties** window and then check the option **Enable writes caching on the device.**

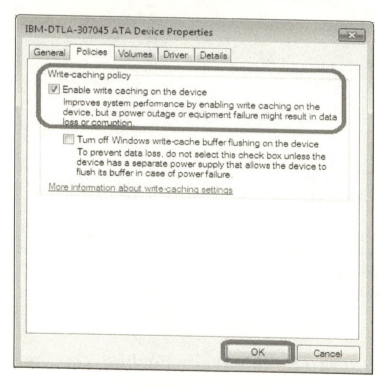

Hard Drive Policies

Make Unneeded Services Manual

By default, some processes that are not necessary automatically start when Windows loads. Users may choose to set these processes to manual since they consume RAM or processor's memory which may result in slowing other key processes.

How To Set The Unnecessary Processes To Manual

- Right click on the **Computer** icon on the desktop and select **Manage.**
- Click on the **Services and Applications** tab.
- Select the **Services** option and from the new window, carefully select the options that are set by default automatic.
- Right click on the chosen option and then select **Properties.**
- In the **startup option,** you can set the services to **Manual** and click **OK.**

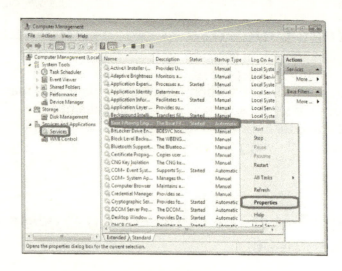

Services and Application Options

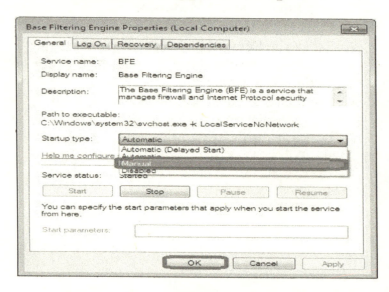

Service and Application Settings

Speedup Window Boot Times

By default, Windows uses one processor to boot the system. Users can decrease the boot time by using the maximum numbers of cores available.

How User Can Decrease The Boot Time

Click on the **Start** button.

Type **"msconfig"** in the windows search box.

Select the **Boot** tab and click on the **Advanced** option.

System Configuration

Check **Number of processes** and enter the maximum number of processors your computer has like 2, 4 or 8.

Click **OK** to apply and **Reboot** the system.

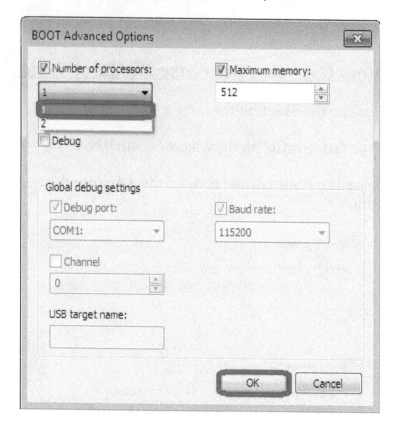

Boot Advanced Option

Chapter 4: How To Speed Up Windows XP

Speed Up Folder Browsing

Users using the Windows XP may have noticed a slight delay when they open My Computer to search a folder. The common reason behind this delay is that the Windows automatically searches for network files or folders every time Windows Explorer is opened.

How To Fix Problem Regarding Delayed Opening Of Folders

- Open the **My Computer** icon placed on the desktop.
- Select **Tools** to open the tools menu and then click on the **Folder Option.**
- Click on the **View** tab and uncheck the option **Automatically search for network folders and printers.**
- Click **Apply** and **Reboot** your system.

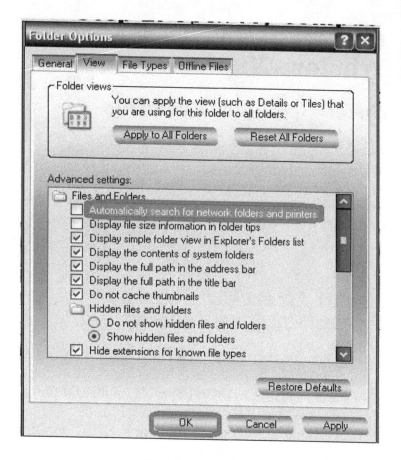

Folder Option

Disable The Performance Counter Feature

Windows provides several tools to measure the performance of the system and display the result in graphical format. Users who do not need this information may disable this service to speed up their system.

The easiest way to disable such measurement tools is to download Microsoft's Extensible Performance Counter List.

Utilize The NTFS File System

It is suggested by the experts that Windows XP should utilize the NTFS system for enhanced performance, reliability and superior security. The computer works either with FAT 32 or NTFS.

How To Switch System To NTFS

- Click on **Start** button and type **CMD** in the windows search box.
- At the prompt, type **CONVERT C: /FS: NTFS** and press the **Enter** key.
- The bootable drive will take a while to convert into NTFS system.

Command Line Interface

How To Check The File Type Of Their System

Double click on **My Computer** and then right click on the **C drive.**

Click on **Properties.**

In the next opening window, the user will see the file system type.

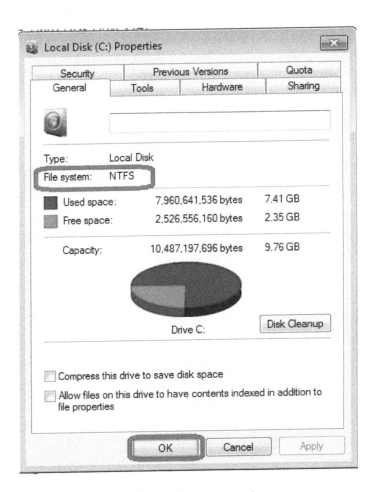

Hard Disk Properties

Empty The Windows Prefetch Folder

Windows XP automatically starts loading the programs that are most frequently or recently used by the user in the Prefetch folder. Although it helps to load the program without any delay it may also use a great deal of memory if it has saved unnecessary programs which are no longer in use.

How The Users May Safely Delete The Contents Of The Folder

Double click on **My Computer** and then click on the **C drive.**

Select the **Windows** folder and then right click on the **Windows Prefetch** folder in the next opening folder.

Select all the files or specifically select the files you don't need in future.

Delete all the unnecessary files.

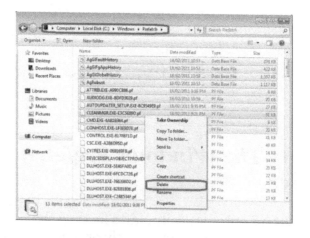

Windows Prefetch

Adjust Processor Scheduling Setting

Users are able to optimize the performance of Windows XP by prioritizing the resources between the foreground programs and the background services.

You may adjust how Windows manages these resources by prioritizing them between the foreground programs and the background services. When the settings are optimized in this manner, it will have a major impact on the overall PC performance.

How To Change The Performance Of Foreground And Background Programs.

Click **Start** and then select **Run** and then type **sysdm.cpl** in the open box.

In the opening **System Properties** dialog box, select the **Advanced** tab. Then under **Performance** tab, Click on **Setting.**

Again, click the **Advanced** tab and choose **Processor Scheduling Settings.**

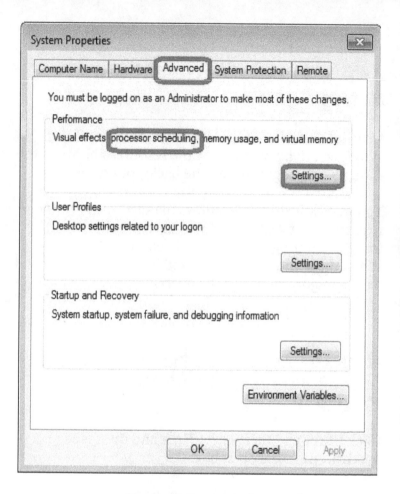

System Properties

Click **Programs** to assign more resources to the foreground programs or Click **background services** to assign equal amount of processor resources.

Click **OK.**

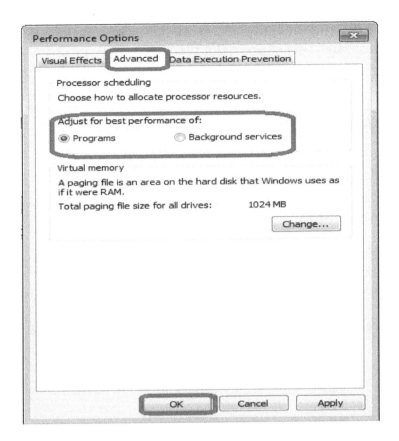

Performance Option

Disable 8.3 Filenames To Reduce NTFS Overhead

NTFS uses 8.3 filenames for compatibility with MS DOS and with some of the older programs. These files are named with eight characters along with a three-character file extension. You can reduce NTFS burden by deleting such files if you are not using any old programs that support 8.3 filenames.

How To Disable 8.3 Files System

Type **"regedit"** in the **Run** dialog box.

Navigate to **HKEY_LOCAL_MACHINE** and move to **System.**

Afterwards, Navigate to **Current Control Set** and click on the **Control** and further select the **File system.**

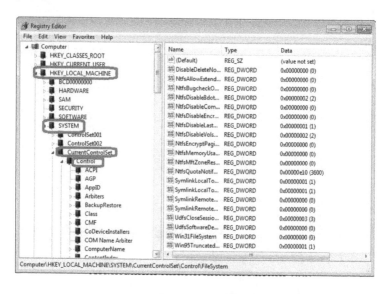

Registry Editor

Find the **NtfsDisable8dot3NameCreation** and modify the value to **1** to disable the creation of 8.3 files name.

Click **Ok** to apply the change.

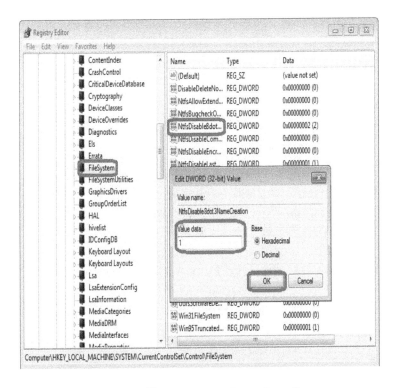

NTFS File Name8.3 Option

Some Additional Tactics To Boost The Performance Of Windows XP

Windows XP provides multiple built in utilities to enhance the performance of the programs which are offered with Windows 7. These services produce the same result but may have little variation when applied to Windows XP. You will see an incredible difference in the speed of computer after following the first twelve tactics mentioned in chapter 3, i.e.:

- Remove Unwanted Programs
- Defragment the Hard Drive
- Remove PC Junk
- Turn Off Visual Effects
- Disable the Search Indexing Feature
- Disable Undesired System Sounds
- Disable Unwanted Start up Items
- Turn Off Windows Screen Savers and Wallpapers
- Disable the Aero Peek and Aero Snap Feature
- Disable the User Account Control
- Remove Undesired Fonts
- Optimize Page Filing of the System
- Set up the Ready Boost Services

Chapter 5: How To Speed Up Windows Vista

Disable Welcome Center

Windows Vista is equipped with the Welcome Center utility to help the beginner easily configure their new computer. It becomes unnecessary with the passage of time. Users may conserve resources by disabling this feature thus boosting the performance of their computer.

How To Disable The Welcome Center Utility

- Click on the **Start** button and type "regedit" in the start search box.
- In the opening window, move to **HKEY_CURRENT_USER.**
- Click on the **Software** then move to **Microsoft.**
- In the newly opened window, Click on **Windows** and then move to **Current Version** and afterwards navigate to **Run.**
- Right click on the **Windows Welcome Center** key and select Delete.

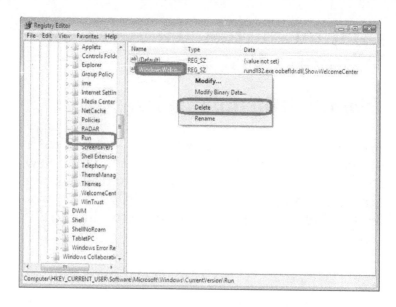

Windows Welcome Center Option

Speeding Up Start Menu Search

When the user enters text in the start search box to locate any file or application then windows by default begins searching for the file index placed on the hard drive. This process can be quite lengthy and time consuming.

How to Save Time And Speed Up The Search

- Go to the **Start** menu and click on Run.

- In the **Run** dialog box, type **"regedit"** and press enter.
- Click on **HKEY_CURRENT_USER** and move to **Software.**
- Navigate to **Microsoft** and expand the **Windows** and then select **Current Version.**

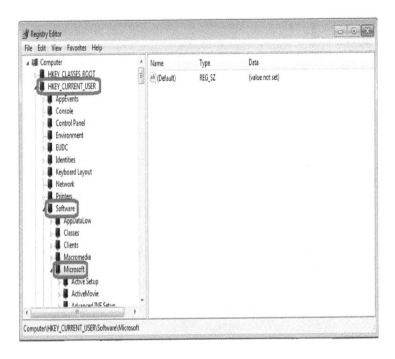

Registry Editor

Click on **Explorer** and then select **Advanced.**

In the next pane of the window, find and right click on the **Start Searchfiles.**

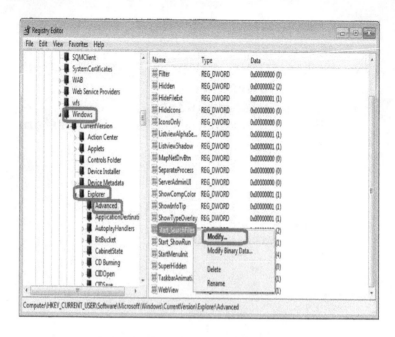

Start Menu Search Option

Move to **Modify** and in the opening dialog box, **set the value to 0.**

Click **OK** and restart your computer.

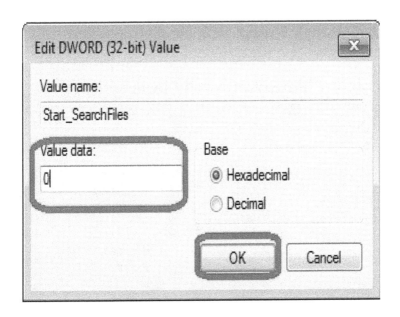

Values Setting of Start Search Menu

Windows Hibernation

Windows Hibernation also uses a large amount of resources. Users are able to boost the performance of their computer by disabling the windows hibernation feature if they don't use it.

<u>*How To Disable The Windows Hibernation*</u>

Click on the **Start** button and then navigate to **Control Panel.**

Go to **Power Option** and click **Change Plan Settings.**

Click on **Change Advanced Power settings** and expand the **Sleep** selection.

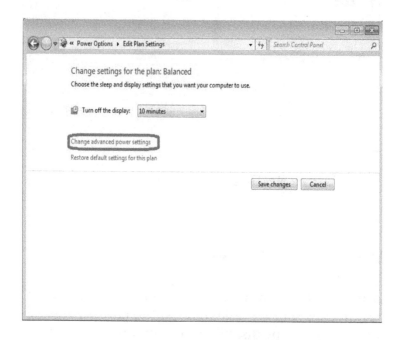

Power Plan Settings

Expand **Hibernation** after selecting and enter zero value in the box.

Click **Apply.**

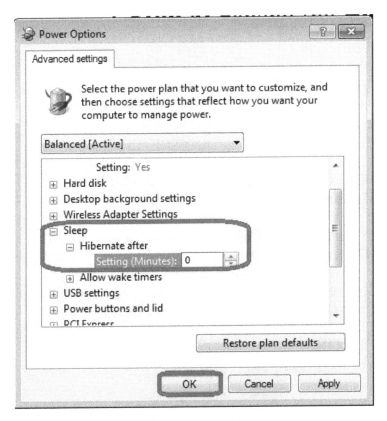

Power Hibernation Settings

Enable DMA For IDE Drivers

If using a system with the IDE drive then it is necessary to enable DMA (Direct Memory Access) mode to smooth the performance of the system.

How To Set Up The DMA

Right Click on **My Computer** and move to **Properties.**

Select the **Hardware** tab and select **Device Manager.**

Expand the **IDE Controllers** and double click the **IDE primary drive**.

Choose the **Advanced** tab and under the **Device Properties** tab, check the option **Enable DMA.**

Click **OK.**

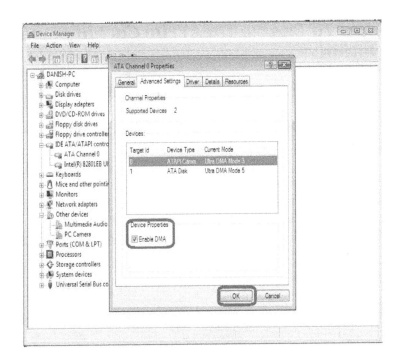

Device Properties

Speed Up External Hard Drive

Users may enhance the performance of their system by enabling the Write caching on the disk option if he/she does not disconnect the external drives frequently.

How To Enable The Write Caching Option

Right click on **Computer** and select **Manage.**

Navigate to **Device Manager** and then expand the **Disk Drives.**

Find the external device and right click on it and select **Properties.**

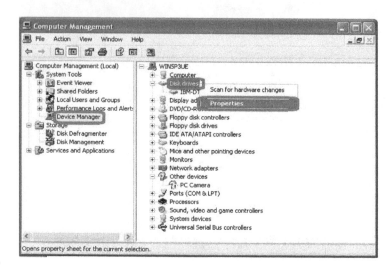

Computer Management Window

Choose the Policies tab and then select **optimize for performance.**

Check the **Enable Write Caching on the Disk** and then enable **Advanced Performance.**

Select **OK** and restart your **PC.**

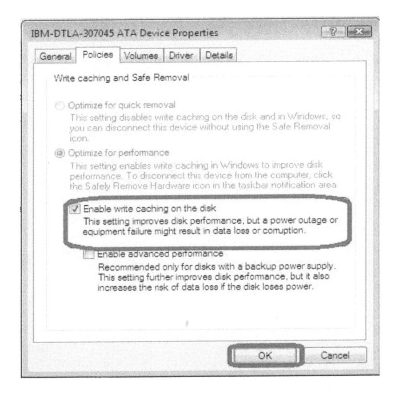

Policies Options

Additional Tactics To Boost The Performance Of Windows Vista

Similar to Windows XP, Windows Vista also shares some of the procedures with Windows 7 which speed up the computer. These procedures are similar for both Windows Operating Systems with few variations in the required steps.

- Remove Unwanted Programs
- Defragment the Hard Drive
- Remove PC Junk
- Disable Unwanted Start up Items
- Disable the User Account Control
- Optimize Page Filing of the System
- Set up the Ready Boost Services

Chapter 6: How To Improve Other Versions Of Windows

This section includes set of tactics that are useful to other operating systems, particularly to the earlier versions of Windows Operating Systems such as 95, 98 or 2000. A brief explanation of the tactics to follow:

Disabling File Last Access Time Check

The earlier versions of Windows OS automatically update the last accessed time of a file which increases the CPU overhead of virtualization. If it is not necessary to the application to use the last accessed time on a server, then user should disable these updates registry key.

Remove Application Runnings At Startup

Users may save a time by removing the applications which begin at startup. This will not remove the entire program from the hard disk but stop it from running at boot time. You may manually start these files whenever required. To remove these programs, you need to right click on the programs and select Delete.

Adjust Virtual Memory Settings

Almost all versions of Windows OS support virtual memory to supplement the computer RAM. By using virtual memory, windows is able to provide extra resources to enhance the performance and capability of your computer.

The following steps are used to change the virtual memory setting:

Step 1: Right click on the **MY Computer** icon placed on the desktop.

Step 2: Click on **Properties** and in the next opening window, select the **Performance** tab.

Step 3: Select **Virtual Memory** and check the option **Let me specify my own virtual memory settings.**

Step 4: Select the hard disk you want to utilize as virtual memory and assign the minimum and maximum amount for it.

Step 5: Click **Ok** and restart your computer.

Clean the Desktop

Users are advised to delete all the unwanted icons and shortcuts and the quick launch bar for program that are placed at the desktop. Every time windows loads, it looks for the contents of these shortcuts which causes a delay.

Chapter 7: General Tactics to Improve System Performance

This section contains the general tactics which will improve the performance of any operating system. This set of tactics works well and is equally useful for a single user PC to high end large computers.

Install Some RAM

The simplest way to enhance the performance of the computer is by adding more RAM. If your system is using 128MB or 256MB RAM then you can upgrade it to 512MB quite easily. Although this procedure will require some investment it is by far the best way to optimize the system performance.

Check Compatibility Of Drivers And Programs

It is necessary to ensure prior to installing new drivers and software that they are compatible with the computer OS. Incompatible software and drivers can cause the system to slow down or in the worst-case scenario to shut down. Prior to installing new software, they should be checked to ensure they are compatible with and support the operating system.

Regularly Examine Your System For Viruses

Viruses are a continual threat associated with computer systems. They may slow down the system by creating additional work for the processors, memory and disks. Almost all the versions of Windows OS offer built in utilities to scan for viruses and other threats. However, users may also run virus checks and clean viruses by using free download antivirus software such as Microsoft Security Essential.

Remove The Dust And Debris From Your Computers

People often ignore the outer working of the computers such as removing dust from the hardware devices, cables, etc. It is highly encouraged by professionals to regularly inspect the computer as the dirt and debris can cause it to slow down when pulled inside by the fan.

How To Make Your Computer Clean Externally

- Unplug your computer and disconnect all the cables.
- Vacuum the external casing of the computer. Never use vacuum inside the computer casing.
- Clean the internal components carefully with the help of small bursts of compressed air.

- Wipe all the dust from the cables, plug heads and the slots with a line free cloth or compressed air or by using tweezers before reconnecting the cables.

Turn Off Password Protection

If you are the single user who uses the computer it is recommended to turn off the password protection which will save the time used in typing the password each time you log on to windows.

Visit Manufacturer's Websites For Updates

For optimized performance, users should regularly visit the official websites of their manufacturer for updates. Users may also download many optional software updates to improve the performance of their computers at their discretion.

Run Fewer Programs At The Same Time

It is also stated by the IT professionals that frequent changes in your computing behavior will have a great impact on performance of your computer. Operators should avoid opening dozens of applications and browsing windows at once to optimize the performance of the computer. It may require some planning to utilize the computer resources in a more optimized method.

Try Free Software Downloads

Currently there are dozens of free download software programs available to boost the performance of the computer. Users may easily make use of such software to enhance the performance of their computer, by choosing software which is compatible to the operating system which is offered by different vendors or manufacturers either for free or at very inexpensively.

Some examples of free download software include Cacheman, Free Registry Cleaner, Advanced system care, Microsoft Security Essential, etc.

Conclusion

Undeniably, computers are an incredible machine of this age. Like all the machines though, they require maintenance on a regular basis to keep them in the top form. If a computer is operating slowly it becomes annoying and frustrating to the user because it takes so long to perform simple tasks. Almost every user experiences these problems after several months of continuous usage.

Tweaking Windows on a regular basis is essential to obtaining optimized performance of the computer. The set of steps mentioned in this guide will certainly help you to eliminate problems and keep your computer operating smoothly. Once you begin using these tactics on a regular basis, it will require less time.

Recommended Resources

- HowExpert.com – Quick 'How To' Guides on All Topics from A to Z by Everyday Experts.
- HowExpert.com/free – Free HowExpert Email Newsletter.
- HowExpert.com/books – HowExpert Books
- HowExpert.com/courses – HowExpert Courses
- HowExpert.com/clothing – HowExpert Clothing
- HowExpert.com/membership – HowExpert Membership Site
- HowExpert.com/affiliates – HowExpert Affiliate Program
- HowExpert.com/writers – Write About Your #1 Passion/Knowledge/Expertise & Become a HowExpert Author.
- HowExpert.com/resources – Additional HowExpert Recommended Resources
- YouTube.com/HowExpert – Subscribe to HowExpert YouTube.
- Instagram.com/HowExpert – Follow HowExpert on Instagram.
- Facebook.com/HowExpert – Follow HowExpert on Facebook.